A DORLING KINDERSLEY BOOK

Conceived, edited, and designed by DK Direct Limited

Note to parents

What's Inside? Boats is designed to help young children understand some of the fascinating details of all kinds of boats. It illustrates what is inside a tugboat, how a paddle steamer works, and what you find below the decks on a motor yacht. It is a book for you and your child to read and talk about together, and to enjoy.

Designers   Juliette Norsworthy and Sonia Whillock
Typographic Designer   Nigel Coath
US Editor   B. Alison Weir
Editor   Sarah Phillips
Design Director   Ed Day
Editorial Director   Jonathan Reed

Illustrator   Richard Manning
Photographers   Matthew Ward and
the National Maritime Museum, London
Writer   Alexandra Parsons

Models supplied by John Bertola,
Tony Olliff, Ted Taylor and Euromodels

First American Edition, 1992

10 9 8 7 6 5 4 3 2 1

Dorling Kindersley, Inc., 232 Madison Avenue
New York, New York 10016

Copyright © 1992 Dorling Kindersley Limited, London.

Library of Congress Cataloging-in-Publication Data
Boats. – 1st American ed.
   p.   cm. – (What's inside?)
Summary: Describes the functions and inner workings of various kinds
of boats, including the rowing boat, cargo boat, and racing yacht.
ISBN 1-56458-006-7
1. Boats and boating – Juvenile literature.
[1. Boats and boating.]   I. Dorling Kindersley, Inc.   II. Series.
VM150.B595   1992
623.8'202 — dc20   91–58216
                                                              CIP
                                                              AC
Printed in Italy

WHAT'S INSIDE?

BOATS

DK

DORLING KINDERSLEY, INC.
NEW YORK

ROWBOAT

This boat is for splashing around on a river or lake. It moves along when the oars are dipped in and out of the water. The rower pulls against the weight of the water to make the boat go forward.

The flat back end of a boat is called the stern.

Oarlocks are the U-shaped hooks that hold the oars in place.

The rudder is used to steer the boat. The rudder is turned to the left or the right by pulling a rope.

This is the keel. It runs from the back to the front of a boat, holding everything together.

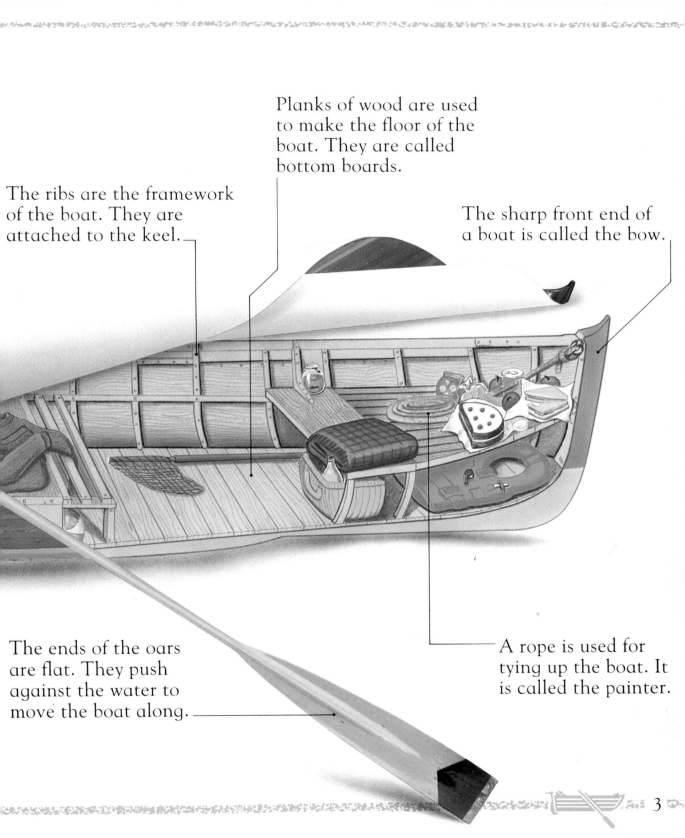

Planks of wood are used to make the floor of the boat. They are called bottom boards.

The ribs are the framework of the boat. They are attached to the keel.

The sharp front end of a boat is called the bow.

The ends of the oars are flat. They push against the water to move the boat along.

A rope is used for tying up the boat. It is called the painter.

3

CARGO BOAT

This is an old-fashioned cargo boat that once sailed up and down the Mediterranean coast, in and out of harbors and ports. It was loaded with barrels of wine, flour, fruit, and other goods.

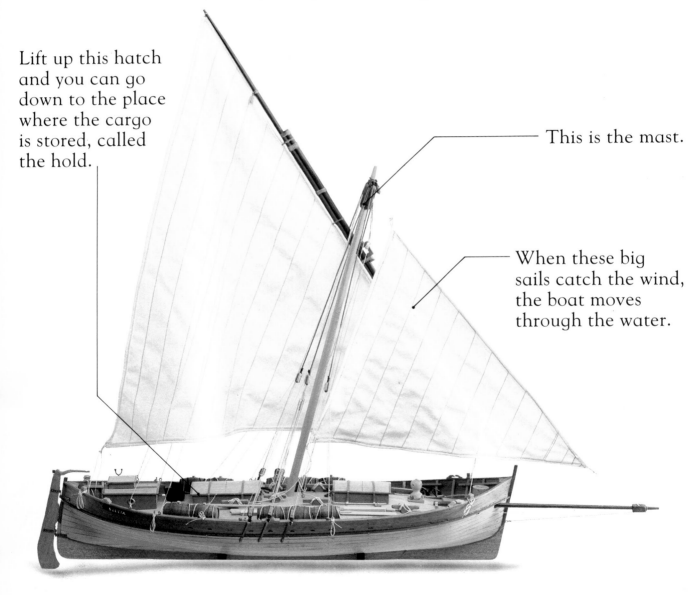

Lift up this hatch and you can go down to the place where the cargo is stored, called the hold.

This is the mast.

When these big sails catch the wind, the boat moves through the water.

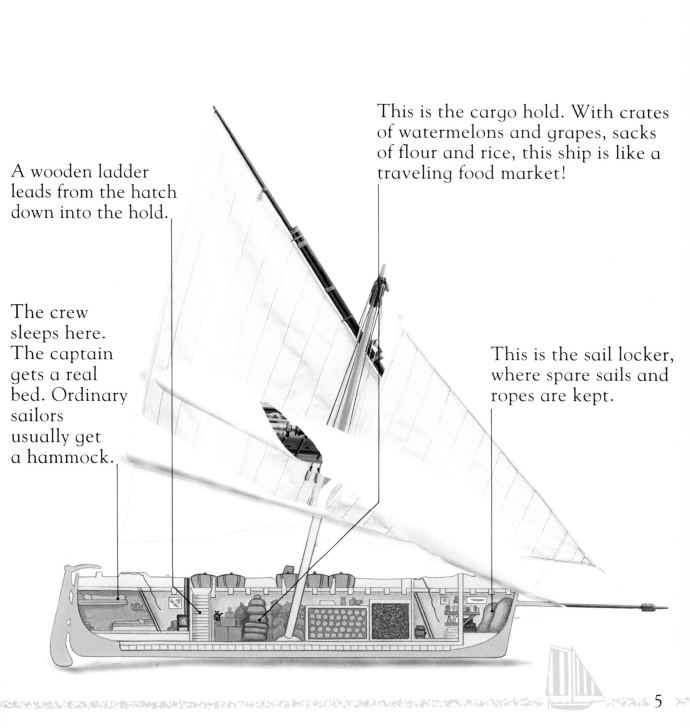

This is the cargo hold. With crates of watermelons and grapes, sacks of flour and rice, this ship is like a traveling food market!

A wooden ladder leads from the hatch down into the hold.

The crew sleeps here. The captain gets a real bed. Ordinary sailors usually get a hammock.

This is the sail locker, where spare sails and ropes are kept.

RACING YACHT

This sailboat is built for racing across oceans. It is long and thin. Its huge billowing sails catch the wind that sends it speeding through the water.

Spare sails are stored beneath this hatch.

A tall mast supports the sails.

This is the yacht's hull. It is made of fiberglass and is very light and strong.

These rails prevent the crew from slipping overboard.

The sails of this racing yacht are much bigger than the boat.

The crew members keep their clean, dry clothes in these lockers. Everything has to be stashed away very neatly to save space.

The bathroom is so small that you have to sit on the toilet to take a shower!

This is the cabin. Yacht races often last several days, so the crew members take turns sleeping.

The kitchen on a boat is called the galley.

FISHING BOAT

This fishing boat is out in storms and choppy seas every day of the week. It is called a trawler. It drags a big net slowly through the water, catching fresh fish.

This is the propeller. It whizzes around and around, pushing the boat through the water. It is powered by a large engine.

The trawler carries another small boat on board. It is called a lifeboat. The crew would use it if the trawler was sinking.

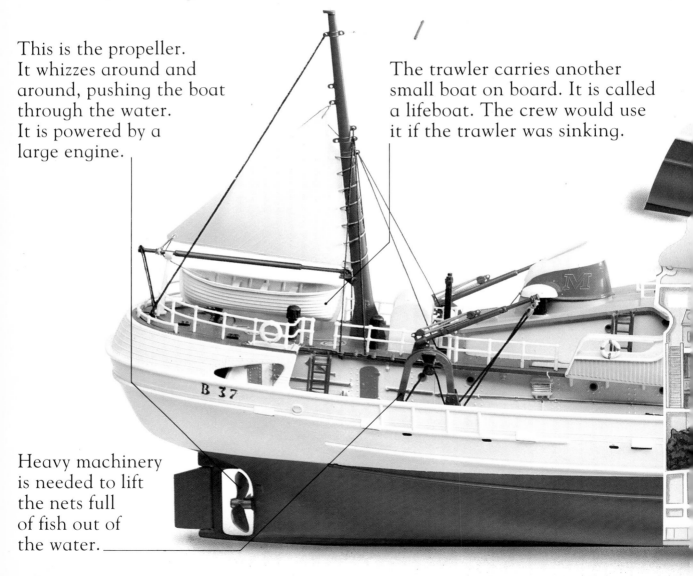

B 37

Heavy machinery is needed to lift the nets full of fish out of the water.

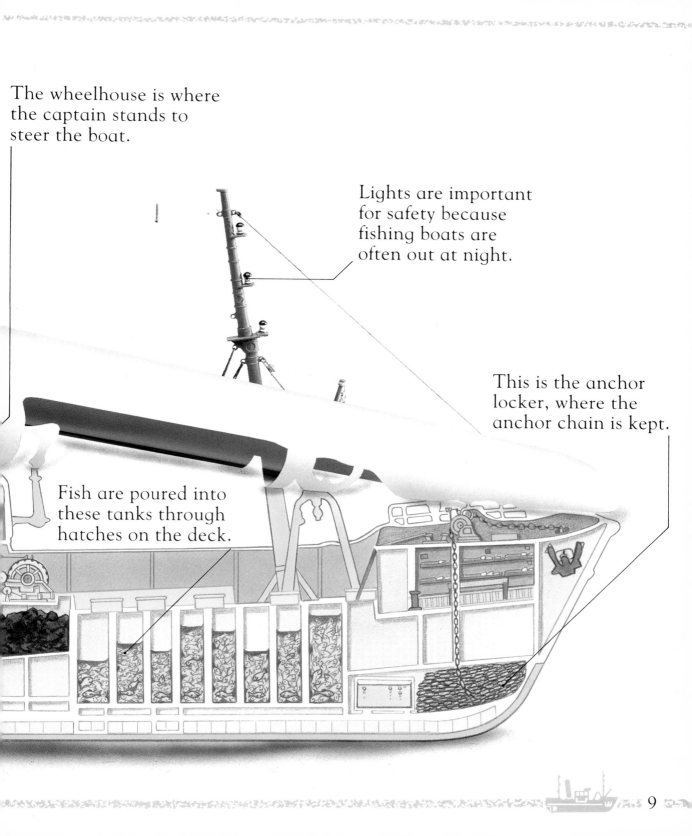

The wheelhouse is where the captain stands to steer the boat.

Lights are important for safety because fishing boats are often out at night.

This is the anchor locker, where the anchor chain is kept.

Fish are poured into these tanks through hatches on the deck.

9

TUGBOAT

Tugs can still be seen working in big ports and harbors. The tugboat's job is to pull and push larger ships in and out of their docks. To do this, tugboats have to be very strong and easy to steer.

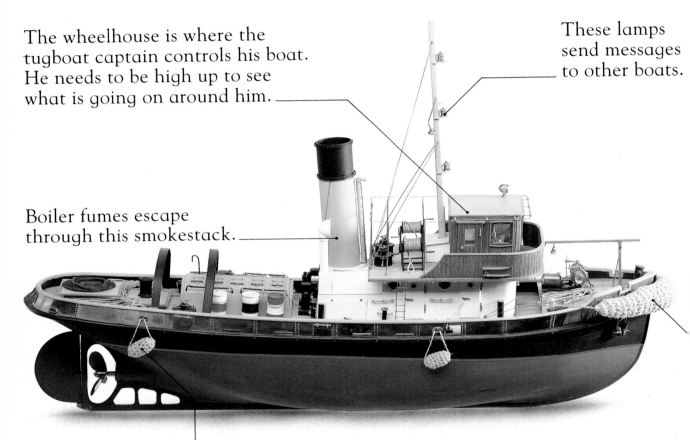

The wheelhouse is where the tugboat captain controls his boat. He needs to be high up to see what is going on around him.

These lamps send messages to other boats.

Boiler fumes escape through this smokestack.

Fenders protect the sides of the tug from bumps and bangs.

Tugs do more pushing than pulling. With this big front fender, a tug can nudge a very large boat into the spot where it is wanted.

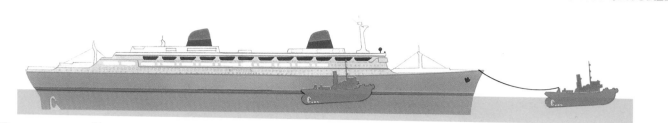

One tug pulls the ship and two others prevent it from swinging from side to side.

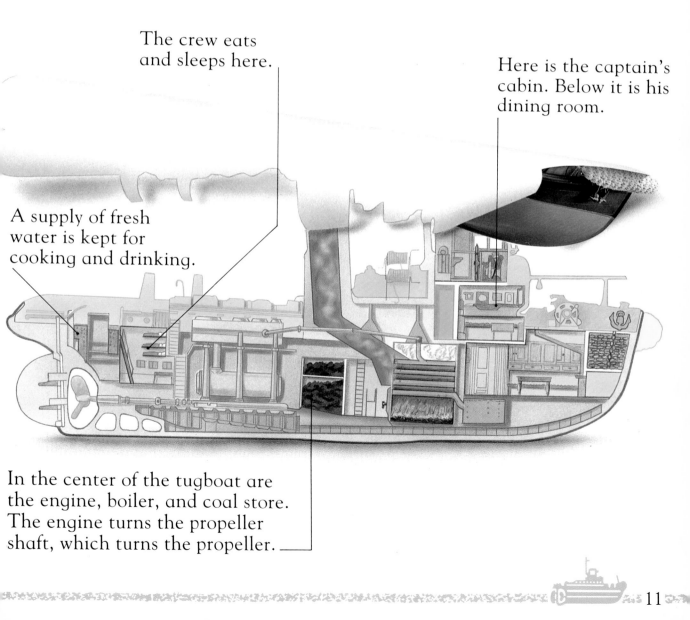

The crew eats and sleeps here.

Here is the captain's cabin. Below it is his dining room.

A supply of fresh water is kept for cooking and drinking.

In the center of the tugboat are the engine, boiler, and coal store. The engine turns the propeller shaft, which turns the propeller.

PADDLE STEAMER

Rivers were once major traffic routes, much like highways are today.
A hundred years ago, boats like this steamed up and down the
Mississippi River, taking people and cargo from one town to another.
A few still travel the river on pleasure cruises.

As the paddle wheel moves
around, the paddles push the
boat through the water.

These cables
support the
smokestacks.

Passengers can walk
around these decks,
enjoying the fresh air
and river views.

The life belts are easy
to find, in case anyone
falls overboard.

Some passengers only stay on board for a few hours, just going to the next town. Others travel for several days.

The passengers are all well taken care of. There are bedrooms, comfortable lounges, and dining rooms on board.

The cargo hold is full of big bales of cotton.

The steam engine drives the chain that moves the paddle wheel around and around.

LIFEBOAT

This boat saves lives. It can travel fast in bad weather and keep steady in stormy seas. Lifeboat crews are specially trained to rescue people from the sea and from sinking ships.

The hatches on deck are watertight so that all below stays dry in rough seas.

A boat hook is used to reach out to small boats or people in the water.

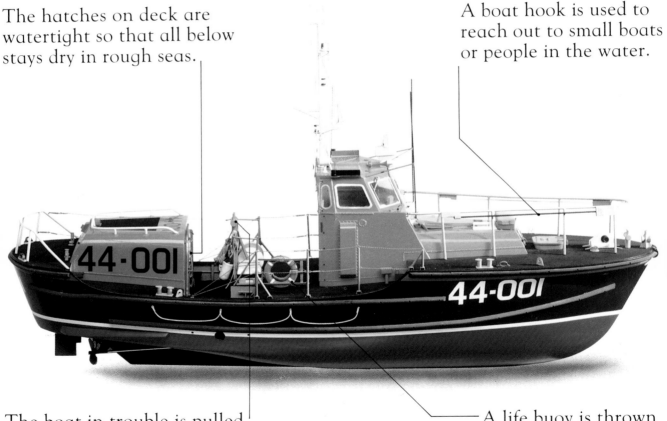

The boat in trouble is pulled along with the towing line, which is attached here.

A life buoy is thrown to people in the water

Lifeboats are very carefully designed. If they turn over in rough seas, they are able to quickly turn back upright.

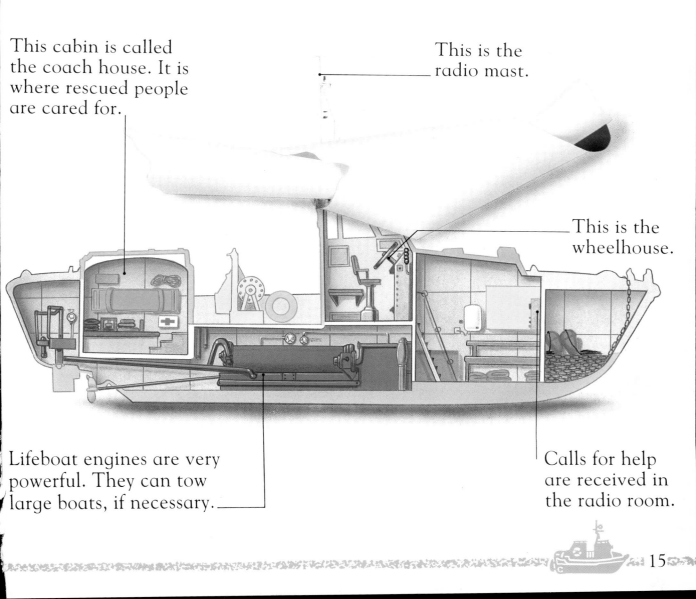

This cabin is called the coach house. It is where rescued people are cared for.

This is the radio mast.

This is the wheelhouse.

Lifeboat engines are very powerful. They can tow large boats, if necessary.

Calls for help are received in the radio room.

MOTOR YACHT

This boat is designed for cruising in warm, sunny weather.
Guests invited on board may simply relax and enjoy themselves.

A speedboat can be lowered into the sea for waterskiing, visiting shore, or exploring beaches.

This is the bridge. When it is raining, the captain sits in here to steer the boat.

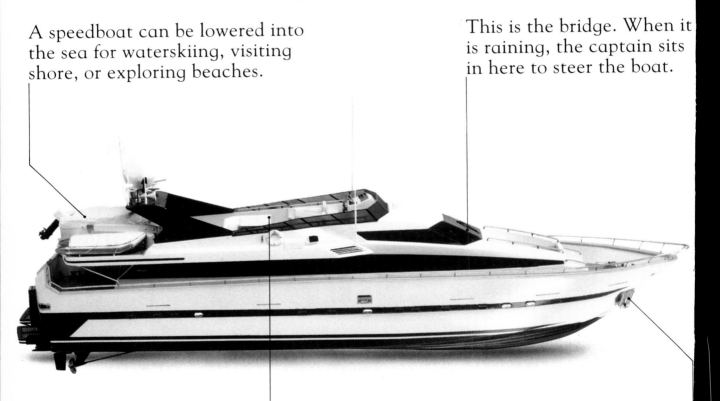

This open top deck is where the captain steers the boat in good weather. The guests can sit and sunbathe.

Here is the anchor. It will be dropped if the guests want to stop for a swim!

Equipment on board includes radar, which can sense other vessels around corners and in the dark. This helps the captain steer at night and in foggy weather.

This is the biggest bedroom. A spiral staircase leads up to the bar and dining room.

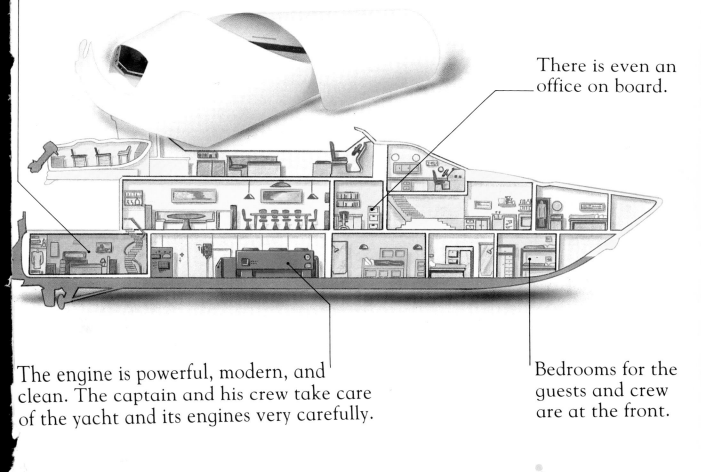

There is even an office on board.

The engine is powerful, modern, and clean. The captain and his crew take care of the yacht and its engines very carefully.

Bedrooms for the guests and crew are at the front.